Hell is Greedy For Souls

Daphne Y. Mitchell

Hell is Greedy For Souls!

"THE SADDEST ROAD TO HELL IS THE ONE THAT RUNS UNDER THE PULPIT, PAST THE BIBLE, AND THROUGH THE MIDDLE OF WARNINGS AND INVITATIONS."

J. C. RYLE

Scripted by Daphne Y. Mitchell

Hell is Greedy For Souls

Trilogy Christian Publishers A Wholly Owned Subsidiary of Trinity Broadcasting Network

2442 Michelle Drive Tustin, CA 92780

10 9 8 7 6 5 4 3 2 1

Library of Congress Cataloging-in-Publication Data is available.

ISBN: 978-1-64773-628-6

E-ISBN: 978-1-64773-629-3

DEDICATION

Joshua, you are one of the best gifts that God has ever given me. It is my prayer that as you live in this earth, that God will reveal Himself to you and that you will be used greatly for Him.

Of all that I could ever give you, the most treasured possession I have is the Word of God. If you want to have good success and if you want to live for all eternity with God, you will have to make the choice to give God your whole heart. You must work out your own salvation with God; this book is birthed in me because of my love for God and my love for you, son. I cry day and night to God for the saving of your soul and for you to be redeemed. May God hear and answer my prayers concerning you. This is the Scripture that God gave me concerning you and me when I was at a crossroad in my life and I did not know which way to turn. I pray that you draw wisdom, understanding, and knowledge from it; it is Isaiah chapter 54, the whole chapter is to be read and remembered.

I love you!

Mom

FORWARD BY AUTHOR

And the devil that deceived them was cast into the lake of fire and brimstone, where the beast and the false prophet are, and shall be tormented day and night forever and ever.

And I saw a great white throne, and him that sat on it, from whose face the earth and the heaven fled away, and there was found no place for them. And I saw the dead, small and great, stand before God; and the books were opened: and another book was opened, which is the book of life: and the dead were judged out of those things which were written in the books, according to their works. And the sea gave up the dead which were in it: and death and hell delivered up the dead which were in them: and they were judged every man according to their works. And death and hell were cast into the lake of fire. This is the second death. And whosoever was not found written in the book of life was cast into the lake of fire.

Revelation 21:10-15

Jesus is the open door, the only truth and the only way, He is the great light that we must accept to be saved. Hallelujah!

ACKNOWLEDGEMENTS

I acknowledge you, Lord, and I trust you to direct my path! For my times and seasons are in your hand. Hallelujah!

Next, I would like to acknowledge and say thank you to my Mom, who is my strongest supporter and truest of friends. I constantly lean on her for wisdom and could not have a better mother if I invented her myself. Thank you, Mother, for setting me on the path of righteousness from my youth as the Lord commands of parents. Your rod of correction proves your love for me. May God keep and bless you richly.

To my son Joshua, who is a God sent, and a joy to

my very existence. Joshua, you are a constant reminder of just how good God is to me! Your very existence echoes an answered prayer request done in secrecy and God's love towards me in public as you are the manifestation of the prayer of a barren woman! I fasted nine days for you and God blessed mightily! May the Lord forever bless and keep you. The Lord anoint and use you for His glory and then receive you to Himself in that great getting up day. May your name be written in the Lamb's Book of Life! Amen!

To my son's dad and his family, I would not even know how to properly love without having a family like yours to show me for 25 plus years. Son's dad, you have been my steady friend and co-parent in this earth and although we are no longer married, you will always be my family! May God cause His face to shine upon you and this family, forevermore.

To Beverly Wright-Powell, my oldest and dearest friend, my sister in the Lord, I would not have been planted in the things of God correctly without you! 1989 was the year of Salvation for me because You were obedient to God! I love you very much and always will! May a star be in your crown of righteousness for the souls you have labored for in this life, which includes mine.

And before I finish, to Sebrena, my beanie! A constant friend and sister! I do not know what I did to deserve you, but I cannot thank God enough for you. A true friend, and a beautiful soul, I pray God gives you every good desire of your heart.

To the few faithful ministers of God in my life who have watched over my soul and prayed and preached me into a sanctified life, I salute your legacies! The late, Bishop

Nicholas Bolton, the late priest of God, Frederick Wilkinson, and the late Bishop Anthony McFarlane.

And finally, to all of you that were so carefully chosen to hurt and hinder me; to my enemies and my frenemies, thank you for keeping me close to God, who is my very great and exceeding reward!

INTRODUCTION

As a witness of Jesus Christ, if I do not ever offend you, it is because I have deceived you. A true witness of Jesus Christ cannot tell the truth of God without people at some point or another getting offended. There are times that the truth of the Bible will cut all of us. But whether offended or not, the Bible is the only true manual that we have for life and death. *HELL IS GREEDY For Souls* is birthed from the pain of knowing that people are dying every day and going into an eternal flame with torments because they bucked against a true relationship with God by their refusal to accept Jesus into their lives while they lived.

The word Hell is mentioned more times in the Bible than Heaven. Let us talk about it!

Hell was originally prepared for the diabolical devil and the fallen angels that he took with him when he was kicked out of heaven; Lucifer was his name. Lucifer was an incredibly beautiful angel in heaven, it is said that the workmanship of his tabrets and of his pipes was prepared in him the day that he was created. (Tabrets are like small drums and the pipes are referred to as tubes used for blowing.) Lucifer has the makings of percussion instruments and wind instruments built into his very being. Can you imagine seeing this angel? Moreover, Lucifer was called one of the anointed cherubs that covereth. According to Ezekiel 10:1-22, these cherubs were to give glory and praise to the Lord and although he had chief involvement in the musical worship to God, he messed up. Let me tell you what happened. He saw himself and became lofty! He got high on self-love and pride, and it

forever ruined him! Now, let us fact check these statements

with the word of God.

It is written in the book of Ezekiel 28:17-18 as thus:

> Thine heart was lifted because of thy beauty,
> thou hast corrupted thy wisdom by reason of
> thy brightness: I (God) will cast thee to the
> ground, I will lay thee before kings, that they
> may behold thee.

> Thou hast defiled thou sanctuaries by the
> multitude of thine iniquity of thy traffick;
> therefore will I bring forth a fire from the
> midst of thee, it shall devour thee, and I
> will bring thee to ashes upon the earth in
> the sight of all them that behold thee.So,
> as you can see, Lucifer got in his own way
> and corrupted himself with iniquity, lust,
> and pride! He became so impressed with
> himself that he believed he could take away
> honor and glory from the Almighty God and
> ascend higher than God; and this, my reader,
> is where sin originated! God, who is Holy and
> Sovereign, was not going to have this unclean,
> disrespectful spirit in His house, so He kicked
> Lucifer out of heaven and changed his name
> to "satan," meaning adversary!

Look at what the prophet Isaiah records in the Bible

about the event.

Isaiah 14:12-17,

How art thou fallen from heaven O Lucifer, son of the morning! How art thou cut down to the ground, which didst weaken the nations!

For thou have said in thine heart, I will ascend into heaven, I will exalt my throne above the stars of God; I will sit also upon the mount of the congregation, in the sides of the north.

I will ascend above the heights of the clouds; I will be like the Most High.

Yet thou shalt be brought down to Hell, to the sides of the pit.

They that see thee shall narrowly look upon thee, and consider thee, saying, is this the man that made the earth to tremble, that did shake kingdoms

[t]hat made the world as a wilderness and destroyed the cities thereof, that opened Not the house of his prisoners?Here it is evident that God's original purpose in creating Hell was for this evil and self - seeking spirit. But as you continue to read, you will begin to understand better why God is going to severely blister and destroy the works of this evil angel and his followers with fervent heat and torments forever and ever.

But first, let me show you the set-up of the heavens

so that you too catch a visual glimpse of God's house. You see, contrary to what most people teach, there are three (3) heavens, and some would even teach that there are seven (7) heavens. I will only discuss the three that scripture supports.

The first heaven is where you and I live. And it is taught that the second heaven is where satan and the fallen angels, better known as demons, temporarily reside. Remember, God said that "satan is the prince of the power of the air, the spirit that now worketh in the children of disobedience" (Ephesians 2:2).

And the Heaven of Heavens is where God dwells along with His heavenly host! Whether this is the third or seventh heaven, I choose not to debate.

But, here's what you need to understand, when satan and the angels that partnered with him were kicked out of heaven, he and those fallen angels, now known as demons or unclean spirits, moved into the bodies of people who are called his prisoners, they are his children.

John 8:44, "Ye are of your father the devil, and the lusts of your father ye will do. He was a murderer from the beginning, and abode not in the truth, because there is no truth in him. When he speaketh a lie, he speaketh of his own; for he is a liar and the father of it."

Furthermore, the Bible informs us that those who have rebelled against God are the seed of the devil, so, there are no two ways about it; if you are not submitted and committed to God then you are in rebellion to God.

Can you see that the same evil works of the devil through lust, pride, hatred, and rebellion are also actively working in people that you work with, perhaps are married to and live with, hang with, and in fact, is even in some of you

reading this book? If you cannot see it, it is because your

father, the devil, has blinded you. You need to know right

now that if God did not put up with that evil then, He sure is

not going to put up with it now. However, you should know

that there is an initial remedy for reversing this curse over

your life and my life too. Here it is: Every one of us must

REPENT!

TABLE OF CONTENTS

FIRST PART

THE BEGINNING

It is impossible to serve God if you do not know God! Discover Him now in the mighty and matchless name of Jesus!

The Bible says God is a spirit and they that worship Him must worship Him in spirit and in truth (John 4:24).

We worship God as the King of Kings and Lord of Lords! He alone is the creator and sustainer of the universe and of our lives. God alone is the Sovereign ruler and rightly claims of Himself to be the Great I am that I am. Psalms 103:19 says, "The Lord has established His throne in heaven, and His kingdom rules over all."

1 Timothy 6:15-16 says, "Which in His times he shall shew, who is the blessed and only Potentate, the King of kings, and Lord of lords; Who only hath immortality, dwelling in the light which no man can approach unto; whom no man hath seen, nor can see; to whom be honour and power everlasting. Amen."

God can speak any language and paint Himself into any canvas of life. He rules and over-rules!

God is omnipresent, omnipotent, and omniscient plus way more.

Believe it or not, God is everywhere at the same time. Which means He is Omnipresent! The prophet Jeremiah asked a question. He asked, "Can a man hide himself in a secret place where God cannot see him?" And then with precision stated that God says of himself; I fill the heaven and the earth (Jeremiah 23:24).

There is no crack, hole, crevasse, crease, cave, den, dark spot, or shelter of any kind that I (God) am not present. We cannot escape His presence or His all-seeing eye, there are no secrets kept from Him.

Moreover, God Almighty is Omnipotent, which means that He is all-powerful! He exists with both power and authority, there is no limitation for Him. No one can counsel Him; He's God! God is restraint free; He plants and plucks up, He raises and pulls down, He kills, and He makes alive.

Also, God is Omniscient which means that He is all-knowing. God gave us our knowledge, therefore we cannot out smart Him, in fact His ways are past finding out. There is no scientist that can challenge the knowing's of God. He lays up storehouses in the depth of the seas, he created the

brain to work better than any computer ever made, and He

regenerates us through His own heavenly reboot. While we

trying to figure it out, God has already been there and done

that.Bonus: Our God is the all-sufficient one. The definition

to that means, already met, already answered, and that He

is infinitely able. He is self-existent, and eternal; please

comprehend this. He alone is the creator of all things, so

He does not seek provision or help from us; it is He that has

made us and not we ourselves! We did not elect God and we

sure cannot impeach Him. God is not a man, or the son of

man, and He is bigger than we think; He alone is our hope

and has become our salvation!

Furthermore, you should know Jesus expressly says

that He is God, when He said, "Before Abraham was, I am"

(John 8:58).

Bottom line, God is who He says He is, and there is

no argument with this writer, I just believe Him.

The providence of God means that His invisible hand

orchestrates all things in the world and in the heavens. He

knows the end from the beginning. How you ask? He planned

it or in other words, He predestined all things. Nothing takes

God by surprise! Listen, God does what He pleases and there

is no one that can stop Him. Job 42:2 says, "I know that you

can do all things; no purpose of yours can be thwarted." Even

the prophet Isaiah says centuries later, "God makes known

the end from the beginning, from ancient times, what is still

to come. God says, "My purpose will stand, and I will do all

that I please" (Isaiah 46:10).

As I continue to make my boast in the Lord, let me

tell you that God is Holy, and every knee will bow to Him

and every tongue will confess that He is Lord.

I have no choice but to make mention and exalt His great name because I love Him. He does excellent things; this is known in all the earth. Because God is a spirit, He does not sleep or get weary like us; nor does God hunger. In fact, He says in one scripture that even if He did hunger, He would not ask us for food.

Also, God does not age, but just in case you need a numerical computation, let me tell you that I only have one formula for His age, and it is resolved in this saying; Alpha and Omega, the beginning and the ending. Furthermore, God does not change, there is no shadow of turning in Him. He is from everlasting to everlasting (Malachi 3:6).Moreover, God's reputation proceeds Him; historically, presently, and forevermore, you can count on Him to do just what He said.

He will never let the righteous fall or fail, and He cannot lie.

Reference scripture: Numbers 23:19 says, "God is not a man that He should lie or the son of man that He should repent!"

Daniel 4:35 says, "After witnessing a tremendous miracle, King Nebuchadnezzar wrote to everyone in his empire: "He, the Lord, does as He please with the powers of heaven and the peoples of the earth. No one can hold back His hand or say to Him: What have you done?"

God is more than I could ever describe, but I cannot neglect to mention that God fights! The fight, however, is always fixed because His name is Victory and He never loses!Finally, God is not only the creator of Heaven, but He is the creator of Hell! Choosing His ways are best if you want to live and die in peace.Reader, I admonish you to get to know Him for yourself, and do not delay because you are running out of time. This world is in the beginning stages of birthing pains and she will begin to rock back and forth like a drunken man. We are in the year 2020 and the beginning of sorrows is here!

Where Did GOD Come From?

Again, God is a spirit! The Lord God is one in three: Father, Son, and Holy Ghost. He has no beginning or ending! He is from everlasting to everlasting! Simply put, *He just is*!

Isaiah 40:28 says, "Hast thou not known? Hast thou not heard, that the Everlasting God, the Lord, the Creator of the ends of the earth, fainteth not, neither is weary? There is no searching of His understanding."

The Mighty Act of God when He Robed Himself in Flesh and bowed the Heavens to come down for you and me!

When we understand what God wants from us, let us

give it to Him. God desires a relationship with His creation.

He wants to fellowship with you! He has gone through great

extremes to make you and I aware of His proven love by

wrapping himself up in a robe of flesh and calling it Jesus. He

stepped out of divinity came down to the earth and walked in

humanity for us.

In the beginning was the Word, and the Word was

with God, and the Word was God! John 1:1 says, "And the

Word was made flesh, and dwelt among us, (and we beheld

His glory, the glory as of the only begotten of the Father)

full of grace and truth." So, it is noticeably clear right there

that in the beginning was the Word and the Word was with

God and that the Word was God Himself! John 1:14 says

that same Word was made flesh and came and dwelt among

men and they saw God in the flesh but did not know it! They

looked at the Creator but did not know it! They looked at

the true light but did not know it, much like today, people do

not believe that the children of God are bearers of His light

and His truth. We are rejected, just like He was! Let us go

deeper!

In reading your Bible, please understand that the

first five books are referred to as the Torah or the Pentateuch

which is translated as the five scrolls in the Greek and in

Hebrew it is translated as the law or instructions. So, let us

open the first book, the book of Genesis.

Genesis lets us see God at work through the authority

of His spoken word! He speaks into existence the world in

five days: creating everything out of nothing but His own

creative thought. In other words, He spoke it and it became

what He said! But on the sixth day, God made us! He made

us in His image and after His likeness. Praise God from on

Hell is Greedy For Souls

High!

So, God creates the first man named Adam and the first woman named Eve (Adams wife) and He gives them paradise. Paradise is called the Garden of Eden, but with paradise comes instructions. God sets things in order by telling Adam His expectations and rules and He also gives Adam a job with authority. He tells Adam to dress the garden and to keep it, and which trees to eat from; He said to eat freely of every fruit of the trees but one and he even tells him what would happen if he disobeys His instructions. The Scripture continues to reveals to us that the relationship between God and Adam was going very well until the serpent, who is the devil approached the woman, Eve. That old, satan begins a conversation with her about what God said and like all smooth talkers do, he began to deceive her with a word salad. Mixing up words, he was able to successfully move her from what God said and she ate of

the fruit of the tree that was in the midst of the garden and

she also gave some to her husband, Adam. But, when Adam

ate of that fruit, creation fell, and sin entered the world as

recorded in Romans 5:12.

Look at the subtleness of deceit. Look at this snake

in the garden talking in a man's voice and setting up his evil

and divisive agenda by contradicting the word of God in the

woman's mind. She begins to hold conversations with the

enemy of God. You should know that the Bible carefully

informs us of the many names of the serpent; such as devil,

angel of light, anti-christ, wicked one, dragon, abaddon,

beelzebub, belial and, quite a bit more – and he is truly seen

as a deceiver in Genesis chapter 3.   Okay, buckle your seat,

because now we are seeing the source of sin and wickedness

being deposited in the human realm by a diabolical and

manipulative devil. The devil is an evil schemer, and he hates God, and he hates what God loves. Isn't it hilarious that the people who usually hate us, wish that they were us? The serpent has crept into the minds and hearts of the people that God selected to be His people and now, we see Adam and Eve tainted and separated from the sweet fellowship with God in the Garden of Eden, that's how this ended.

Even today, he continually tries to corrupt and/or contaminate us to do and say the things that break fellowship with God. The manifestation of sin through stealing, killing, lying, living in homosexual lifestyles, and all that is wicked in the sight of God and man. The focused effort of the devil to deceive the whole world which began with the woman, Eve, and her husband, Adam, is at work and God's prized relationship with mankind has seemingly gone south because of sin. But how many of you know the power of love? God

XIII

hates sin, but He loves us !

To the natural eye, this presents somewhat of a dilemma in our finite minds but in God's predetermined plan, He already knew what He was going to do. Now let's be real, God could have easily wiped out everything and everyone and just created the order that He wanted in the earth, but He chose to let man have free-will to serve Him and to choose His ways as opposed to making robots as it were. It's like us in today's world, you don't want to be with someone because they are programmed to be with you, but you want to know that they are with you because they love you, right?

See, all throughout the Old Testament of the Bible, God has shown Himself to be a Holy consuming fire, a rock in a weary land, a cloud of protection, and a man of war, a

Priestly Angel called Melchizedek, who has no beginning or ending, a rescuer, an ark of safety, and so much more. He is such a loving Father who has always desired a relationship with His people but not by force. He wants us to long for Him out of a true and authentic heart!

God is the Creator, but when He created the angels and the host of Heaven, He created them to obey Him. When He created mankind, He gave us free-will to obey or not to obey. He shows us through the lives of different people in the scripture the path of righteousness as well as the acts of unrighteousness. For example, through Moses, He gives us clear instructions that if we want to please Him, then we must follow the ten (10) commandments! It is only ten (10) commandments, people!

These ten commandments fulfill all the laws of God!

But because we are so wicked and selfish, some of us will

not hear and obey. Disobedience is rebelliousness in the eyes

of God, and rebelliousness is the same as witchcraft. Also,

unbelief is a horrible trespass with God! When we act in

unbelief, it is the same as calling God a liar. Have mercy on

us!

SECOND PART

The Ten Commandments

1. *Thou shalt have no other gods before me.* That means,

   do not put anything, any person, or yourself before

   God! Nothing!

   He alone must take first place in all we do, no

   exceptions. If we would do this, the world would be a

   different place and we would be different people.

2. *Thou shalt not make unto thee any graven images,*

   or likeness of anything that is in the Heaven above

   or that is in the earth beneath or that is in the water

   under the earth. That means, don't make any carved

idol of any type of representation of a god to worship.

No buddha, no Mary, no person, no anything!

There is only one God and He is in the heavens

(Deuteronomy 6:4)."Thou shalt not bow down thyself

to them nor serve them, for I the Lord thy God am a

jealous God, visiting the iniquity of the fathers upon

the children unto the third and fourth generation of

them that hate me" (Exodus 20:5). God is saying

that you show Him hate when you provoke Him to

jealousy by carving out an image with your hands to

worship, as if He does not exist! You set up a false

god and I live, says the Lord. I do wonders amongst

you! I created what you carve out and duplicate! I

will visit you and your children's children's children

for this iniquity!" (Exodus 20:5).

(Iniquity means wickedness, willfully sinning, and

evil deeds.)

3. *Thou shalt not take the name of the Lord thy God*

    in vain, for the Lord will not hold him guiltless that

    taketh His name in vain.

    What does that mean?

    God does not want you to profane or make wrongful

    use of His name. Do NOT play around with His

    name! He is not a joke, He is Holy!

    He is not Lawdt or Lordt, those names are Irreverent

    – He is Lord! God Almighty, which was, which is,

    and which is to come! Please forgive us, Lord, for

    taking your name in vain and being disrespectful to

    you. In Jesus name. Hallelujah!

4. *Remember the Sabbath Day, to keep it Holy. Six*

    days shalt thou labour and do all thy work: but the

    seventh day is the Sabbath of the Lord thy God:

in it thou shalt not do any work. No one in your

gates is permitted to do any work either. The Lord

Blessed this day for us to rest in His presence and He

hallowed it!

(Hallowed means: Holy, He made this day sacred.)

5. *Honor thy father and thy mother, that thy days may*

be long upon the land which the Lord thy God giveth

thee. Honor means to Value! Do not depreciate your

relationship with your parents. Be respectful to them,

they either took care of you at one point or still take

care of you; they brought you into this world. It is the

first commandment with promise. If you do not honor

your parents, your days on earth will be shortened,

and that is the promise of God.

6. *Thou shalt not kill.* We are not to take the life of

another person. The first murder in the Bible was

when Cain killed his brother Abel, and God came

down and visited this situation! By the time God

finished with this situation, Cain was a marked cursed

and made to be a vagabond in the earth.

7. *Thou shalt not commit adultery.* Adultery means

unlawful intercourse or sex with the spouse of

another.

It creates a breach in the marriage! God said,

"Thou shalt not." This sin breaks and has broken up

many homes; it ruins the lives of innocent people

in different ways. It creates a high risk for suicide,

diseases that are terminal, mental anguish, financial

burdens, confusion, and depression for all in involved.

Children really suffer in a lot of these cases.

8. *Thou shalt not steal.* Steal means to take another

person's property without permission or legal right

and without intending to return it.

This is what people who hate you do. They operate

out of the spirit of the wicked one! It is the devil who

comes to steal, kill, and destroy, and his children are

just like him. Pay attention! Look at who you are

dealing with! Look at what they are doing, listen to

what they are saying! Everyone is wearing a label

of some sort, now look at their contents to see if the

label matches their insides (their heart and actions).

If they do not, its's false advertisement and it is a

liar that you are dealing with! Separate yourself

immediately!

They are of their father, the father of lies, who is the

devil! We see his label and his contents 20/20.

9. *Thou shalt not bear false witness against thy*

neighbor.

False means not true!

Wonders calculated to deceive. Liars! God does

not want us lying on each other. Remember who the

father of lies is? Unless you are the devil's child, we

should not be involved in this at all.

10. *Thou shalt not covet thy neighbor's house, thou shalt*

    not covet thy

    neighbor's wife, nor his manservant nor his ox, nor

    his ass, nor anything that is thy neighbor's. This

    means do not set your desire or intense passion for

    anything that someone else has, like it is yours.

    Get your own! We are not to lust for other people's

    stuff and think that we are entitled to it!

Again, if we would only obey these ten laws, our world

would be heaven on earth and at peace. Our lives would be

elevated to a place of peace most of us have never known.

Obedience is the key! Obedience is better than sacrifice!

By obeying these ten (10) commands, what a life each of us would live, there would literally be no lack, no jealousy, no division, no hatred, no murders, no gossiping because we would be so busy helping each other and pleasing God. All things would go well with us, but that is not the world we know and live in, is it? While it seems bleak, we individually are still responsible for living out these commandments even though our neighbors may choose not to.

THIRD PART

THE REPORT OF THE LORD

There are many reports of truth today according to the world but in the book of Isaiah, a question was asked. The question is, 'whose report will you believe?' The response, if you want to be in right standing with God, must be that we will believe the report of the Lord (Isaiah 53:1).

Many will argue that the King James Version of the Bible is inaccurate and therefore cannot be trusted for salvation and is not necessarily a standard to be used for living, but I declare unto you by the authority of the Holy Ghost that all scripture is given by the inspiration of God. All of

God's scripture is profitable for doctrine, for reproof, for

correction, and for instruction in righteousness, that the

man of God may be perfect, thoroughly furnished unto all

good works (2 Timothy 3:16-17).

Having faith in God's Word is like asking a person to

tell you how an orange, that you are eating, tastes. They

cannot, unless you give them a piece and they taste it too.

God says, "O taste and see that the Lord is good" (Psalms

34:8).We must eat the Word! Amen.

Be sure of this fact, if you do not read and hold the Word

of God in your heart you will never discover the power

of His spoken truths. Sadly, you will never believe His

report.

God is the Word! And He backs up every word that

has been written because it is, He that the written word

speaks of. The Bible is the only book that reveals the

mind, personality, likes, dislikes, reputation, character,

plans, and yes, the punishments and rewards of God. His

mind is revealed to the people of God as well as to the

enemies of God. There will be no excuses!

God has given us 66 books in the Bible to assist us on

our journey here. These books are broken up by Old and

New Testaments in the Bible. From the beginning book of

Genesis to the last book, the book of Revelation, we see

God pleading with us to choose Him, to choose eternal

life in Him! The choice to live and not die – by the way,

there are two lives and two deaths.

The first life is when we arrive through the birthing canal

of our mother, this is the carnal birth. The second birth is revealed through the invitation of God to be born again

and surrender our ways and lives unto Jesus Christ. The

second birth is detailed in John 3:1-7:There was a certain

man of the Pharisees, named Nicodemas, a ruler of the

Jews. The same came to Jesus by night, and said unto

him, Rabbi, we know that thou art a teacher come from

GOD; for no man can do these miracles that thou doest,

except GOD be with him.

> Jesus answered and said unto him, Verily, verily, I say unto thee, except a man be born again, he cannot see the kingdom of God.

> Nicodemus saith unto Him, HOW can a man be born when he is old? Can he enter the second time into his mother's womb, and be born?

> Jesus answered, Verily, verily, I say unto thee, except a man be born of the water and of the Spirit, he cannot enter into the kingdom of God. That which is born of flesh is flesh; and that which is born of the Spirit is Spirit. Marvel not that I said unto thee, Ye must be born again.

Hell is Greedy For Souls

To be born the second time a person must:

1. Believe in their heart that Jesus died on the cross, was buried in the grave, and rose on the third day for their sins.

2. Confess with their mouth that Jesus is Lord.

3. Repent of all their sins – "repent" meaning to have deep regret or remorse about all your wrongdoing in the eyes of God.

4. Forsake those sins.

5. Be Baptized in the name of Jesus (Acts 2:38).

6. Be filled with the Spirit of God – Ask God to come and dwell inside of you and take up His abode.

7. Read and study the Bible while living a committed life with a committed heart to God until you die – get in a Bible-teaching church if you have not already.

Now, the first death is the natural death of the flesh,
but the second death is spiritual, it is when those who die
without God living in them are sealed for the damnation of
their souls. This death is brutal and eternal! This soul will
forever be separated from God, due to their choice. Choosing
to live in sin and never accepting God's way is choosing a
brutal death.

God says, 'I am the Way, the Truth, and the Life, Selah!
(Selah, means to pause and think about it.)

If you are reading this and you are scared, you can
change right now. Follow the steps above; accept God into
your heart and live unto Him.

Yes, having a Godly fear and reverence is good.

If you do not feel the conviction of the Holy Spirit,
you will need the prayers of the saints to assist you in being

xxx

delivered from a stronghold in your life.

Please contact a local church and ask for prayer.

The second death is explained in Psalms 9:17, and it says, "The wicked shall be turned into Hell, and all the nations that forget God."

God warns us that the wages of sin is death, but the gift of God is eternal life in Christ Jesus our Lord (Romans 6:23).

God says in Revelation 21:8, "But as for the cowardly, the faithless, the sexually immoral, sorcerers, idolaters, and all liars, their portion will be in the lake that burns with fire and sulfur, which is the second death."

Now for all those people who say, we are already living in Hell, you are wrong. This place that God mentions is a physical place and you go here after the first death if you are not born again in Christ. Also, in Luke 16:22-23, God

shares with us another report!

One day, two men died, one was rich and had

everything in this life and the other man was a beggar. This

beggar was laying outside the gate of the rich man's house,

but the rich man did not show him any kindness, nor any

compassion while they both lived. In fact, it was a dog that

licked the beggar's sores and relieved him of the pain that he

suffered. Well, as I said, they both died. And in Hell, the rich

man lifted his eyes, being in torments!

This rich man had it good while he lived, he did

not suffer for the need of anything while, like others who

genuinely love and serve God, this beggar went without and

it seemed like just another death. But death is an equalizer,

the redeemed of the Lord get their souls carried by angels

into the very presence of God to live in the bosom of

Abraham until the trumpet of God is blown. This is the first

resurrection, but the souls of those who are evil are turned

into Hell!

Sinners use the reasoning that "God is love and He will not

destroy me." Today, in fact, most people do not even believe

in God anymore because when they sin, it appears that they

do not receive immediate punishment or physically die

during their transgression.

To them it seems like there is no judgment but be

clear: just because judgment is slow, it does not mean that

judgment is not coming. The deception is because we live in

a microwave generation, where everything happens now, but

in the transgressor's mind, "nothing happened to me, so I got

away with my sin!" Everything is not as it seems though!

An appointed time has been set! God says that He has made everything for His purpose, even the wicked for the day of evil (Proverbs 16:4).

Why would a loving God want to burn people with an unquenchable fire?

He does not want to, but He is going to burn the wicked. All of us need to quickly repent and live a reconciled life to God.

Today, it is a shame to say that a lot of churches don't represent the God of the Bible, instead they represent an imagined God that tolerates gay marriages, men and women leaving their covenant marriages discarding each other like rubbish, pastors who think Sunday is their payday, and preachers who drink alcohol, do drugs in their offices, and who are sexually immoral with children and multiple women; defiling themselves and others and who continually bring a reproach on the name of Jesus. Right now, all types of evil

works are happening in the church beginning at the pulpit

straight down to the pews. Churches today have all kinds

of agendas going on inside them and expect that God, who

is Holy, will be among them. For the record, God is about

His purpose, not ours! He requires that we worship Him in

spirit and in truth. As an example of ridiculous things done

by people professing to know God, I ask, "What does the

Easter and Christmas program have to do with God and His

Salvation?" "What does God care about the toy drive for

tots?" The God of the Bible cares about what He has already

made known through the scriptures. Yes, it had to be said!

The people have strayed so far from God that before

God shows up in a church service, we are already gone for

the day. We think that we can just come in and say what we

want God to do, dance at the altar, say a couple of scriptures, and talk about a whole bunch of nonsense before God and assume that He is with us.

He has stipulations! He has rules! He sits on the throne! This generation thinks that God jokes, but He does not!

God sits on the throne and out from His throne goes forth lightning and thunder. There are 24 elders who are constantly bowing and throwing their crowns before Him day and night, crying, "HOLY, HOLY, HOLY!" And there are four living creatures, each with six wings and covered with eyes, around and within. They do not rest day and night, saying, "Holy, Holy, Holy, Lord God Almighty, who was and is and is to come" (Revelation 4:8).

This is not a God that plays around. We are not being taught the God of the Bible and people will be completely caught off guard because the preachers are not sharing

the truth. A lot of them are drowning in sin and wear the

garments of shame; some are even the ministers of satan, and

some only want fame and money for themselves.

Most churches are dismissing church services

without even extending the invitation for people to come and

surrender their lives over to Christ for the sake of getting out

of church on time. My goodness, no one in Heaven is sitting

in the presence of God, chewing gum, writing notes, or trying

to pick up a woman or a man. No! They are worshipping

with great reverence! The church should be in constant prayer

and eating tears daily for God to have mercy.

This book is being written because it is a warning and

an appeal for us to get to know the God of the Bible and to

learn of Him quickly! It is my plea that we spend more time with God and less time with the distractions of this earth. I admonish us to use our time wisely because the days are evil, and we cannot afford to die knowing a fake God who cannot save. We must be intentional about praying to the God of Heaven and seeking Him with our whole hearts as if our very lives depend on it, because our lives and souls really do.

It must be through desperation that we seek Him and find Him. No pride and no shame, but true worshippers are what the Father seeks. He said that if we seek Him with our whole heart that we would find Him.God loves to be worshipped and praised, and why wouldn't he? He has done and continues doing so much for us. We have a real love, the love of God, and we are so undeserving of it.

Just imagine for a minute all the things that God does for not just you, but all kinds of people, all over the globe who have put their trust in Him.

Think, who causes the sun to rise and set, the moon

to shine, and keeps the planets on their axis? Who keeps

the waters from crossing their boundaries and overtaking

mankind? Who controls the seasons?

Who does it?

No one can be compared to our God. No one!

Truth be told, we owe God our everything and we need to

pay up!

I know that most of you work all week and want to

relax on the weekend and especially on Sunday's, but missing

church is not wise. Yes, there is television, tapes, cd's, and

all types of ways to live stream church services, but there

is nothing like being in the very presence of God and His

people in an activated environment that invokes the Spirit of

God to bow down the Heavens and ride His cloud to inhabit

our praise and rescue us. While others of you may be saying

that going to church to be around a bunch of hypocrites

and judgmental people is not how you want to spend your

morning. Either way, missing a chance to be in the very

presence of God is not wise and will not be an excuse to use

when you have to stand before God and give an account to

Him for rejecting to spend time learning about Him. You are

responsible for your own soul.

After all, you and I are always in the presence of

hypocritical people. They are at your job, your gym, your

daycare, your local grocery store, your salon, and at the club

or dance hall.

The fact is, no matter where we go, there will always be

"pretending," but there are also some of us who are very real and are having a true experience with a true God.

Do not die doubting the report of the Lord! Accept the 66

Books of the Bible for your personal guide to God and lay

hold on eternal life! Make sure that your name is written

in the Lamb's Book of Life! Look around you, look at the

reports of the news channels, look at the reports of your

friends and family members, look at the reports of the

doctors, nurses, and healthcare professionals. No salvation

can be found in them. There is only one way, one truth, and

one life – His name is Jesus Christ! Accept Him today.

Daphne Y. Mitchell

FOURTH PART

GOD'S PASSIONATE LOVE

To be honest, God reveals His supernatural love

through His servant Moses in the book of Exodus. The book

of Exodus shows us God organizing the people of Israel to

become His people. He began to show us a typology of what

He was going to step out of Heaven and do for us! Truly,

God came down from the Heavens and took on the form of

man for you and me.

The gospel of John in the New Testament begins by telling us

that

> In the beginning was the Word, and the Word
> was with God, and the Word was God. The

same was in the beginning with God. All
things were made by Him, and without Him
was not anything made that was made. In
Him was life, and the life was the light of
men. And the light shineth in darkness; and
the darkness comprehended it not.

John 1:1-5

See, God came down from Heaven and robed Himself

in flesh, divinity took on the form of humanity and called

himself, Jesus. He was also called Emmanuel, which means

God tabernacles or God is with us.

Jesus walked the earth and taught us how to be like

Him. He taught us how to live, how to have the right attitude,

how to treat one another, and mostly, how to please the

Father. Jesus taught us how to treat His sheep and run His

ministry.

Verse 10 of the same chapter says, "He was in the

world, and the world was made by him, and the world knew

Him not." It is still that way today for many people. People

do not have a clue of who God is and it does not help that we

have so many false witnesses on the earth who use the name

of Jesus for selfish gain. They use His name to make a name

for themselves and to get wealth and notoriety.

But the reason that God came to the earth is for us, who

believe. He died for us! His love for us kept Him nailed

to the cross after being severely beaten with whips, spat

upon, mocked by evil men and women! He called this the

passion of His cross! His love for you and I surpass my

understanding because He allowed them to beat Him until He

was unrecognizable. He bled and died so that you and I could

be redeemed by His spilled blood. His blood purchased our

salvation.

Perfect love hung on an old rugged cross and died

for us! Then our God went into the grave and redeemed all

those who had died believing in Him, and He took the sting

out of dying for the believer and put victory in the grave for

us. When we die, we sleep in Him, unlike the wicked. When

they die, they are tormented and reserved for even worse, the

Lake of Fire, because they rejected His perfect, proven, and

passionate love.

Listen, Jesus is God revealed! The Bible says in John

1:14, "And the Word was made flesh, and dwelt among us,

(and we beheld His glory, the glory as of the only begotten of

the Father,) full of grace and truth.

John 3:13-16 says,

And no man hath ascended to heaven, but he
that came down from heaven, even the Son of
man which is in heaven. And as Moses lifted
the serpent in the wilderness, even so must
the Son of man be lifted up that whosoever
believeth in him should not perish but have
eternal life. For GOD so loved the world that
he gave his only begotten Son, that whosoever

believeth in him should not perish, but have everlasting life.

Romans 5:8-11 says,

> But God commendeth his love towards us, in that, while we were yet sinners, Christ died for us.
>
> Much more then, being now justified by his blood, we shall be saved from wrath through him.
>
> For if, when we were enemies, we were reconciled to GOD by the death of his Son, much more, being reconciled, we shall be saved by his life.
>
> And not only so, but we also joy in God through our Lord Jesus Christ by whom we have now received the atonement.

So, it is clear to see that had it not been for the death, burial, and resurrection of Jesus Christ, no flesh could be saved. His blood became the atonement for our sins.

(Atonement means: The reparation for a wrong or injury.

Reparation means: Repair or Compensation.) Jesus repaired us back to God! He makes us righteous before Him.

So now, let us talk about the love on earth. How many people do you know of or remember hearing them say, I love you? Are they still in your life? If so, do you still feel and see actions that demonstrate to you that their statement is true?

Have you married or made a commitment to a boy/man or girl/woman that declared their love for you, and are they still around? Are they still in your corner today? If not, where are they? Did they keep their promise or vow to you?

I will be the first to confess, I do not know where half of the people who once told me that they "love me" are at in this world today. I do know that I was discarded when people chose to move on to other people and to do what they thought was best for them, and I too, have discarded when I thought that I could or should have better. The words "I love you" are used so loosely and likely are not even true when spoken,

most times. Usually, the love is found to be just lust, which

is why it is so easy to turn our backs on what our mouths

once said.

Love is an intense and deep affection for something

or someone in the dictionary, but in Hebrew, the word love

means "give."

Giving is an act of service. It is no wonder that Jesus

says to the husband, 'lay down your life for your wife.' How

many times do we see this commandment being followed in

the church where the divorce rate is higher than anywhere in

the world?

Love is ventilated through giving. They go hand-in-

hand when it is real, so if we are to measure love, we will see

it extended through our giving. If you are giving and I am

giving, then we know that we love each other. But misuse and abuse enter when we fake love; one person is giving, and one person is taking, and it is never balanced.

God loved and so gave, now we must show God that we love Him back and give our lives to Him and prove our passion, on our cross, and sacrifice our own desires in exchange for His will! Pure and undefiled love is available for you, and I hear the hymnologist singing: When nothing else would help, love lifted me!

The Bible is God's love letter to us! Have you ever read it?

Let me ask you this, have you met a person and through a series of dates with the passing of time, fell in love with that person? What was it that caused you to fall in love with him or her? When you fell in love with them, did you make the first announcement that your heart was in and

L

that your body screams for them? What was the response?

Was the response positive or negative? If it was positive,

then the person most likely responded with an "I love you

too." Perhaps that love blossomed into a marriage and you

are living out the truest expression of your love with that

person, or perhaps, the response was negative. You alone fell

in love and that is why the union of hearts did not manifest

into anything more than wasted time. Your love was rejected!

Your love was unappreciated, undervalued, taken for granted,

and you can tell because why? Because nothing from the

seed of your heart landed into good ground and produced

anything that was good; but rather, pain was produced. Your

heart aches because you do not understand how loving him

or her went wrong and caused you anguish, disappointment,

frustration, and all the negative emotions. It was not

supposed to go this way, right? The truth is that some people will kill themselves because of a bad experience and think

that love can never be found again while others just carry a

broken spirit, a damaged mind that affects every other good

thing that comes into their lives. They never trust anyone

else with their vulnerability. Well....

I have got good news folks, the love of God gives us

the greatest love we will ever know. If our hearts love Him

back, we get to experience Heaven on earth, but if we act like

the person who God has expressed His love to but rejects it,

we will find ourselves in great torments later. No one likes

rejection and can you imagine having someone die for you

to express their love and it not be good enough? Remember,

Jesus was beaten until he was unrecognizable, because He

loved us! His love is revealed on the cross! The passion of

His love was His blood! No one will ever love you like this,

no one! From the book of Genesis to the book of Revelation

in the Bible, we see the love of God and the benefits and

rewards of a healthy relationship with Him. Things may

not have worked out between you and a natural lover in this

life, but with God you are able to experience true love every

moment of every day if you want to. And while God is the

one who instituted Holy Matrimony and says that it is not

good for man to be alone, I encourage all single people to

seek God's direction for marriage and believe that He is able

to provide a ram for your bush if you truly desire a mate.

But do not miss out on God's love while you wait and don't

become desperate and look for love in all the wrong places.

Meanwhile, if you have a mate, love them but do not set them

up above God. God is a jealous God!

Daphne Y. Mitchell

FIFTH PART

POWER OF GOD'S BLOOD

When the Lord Jesus was crucified on the cross, His

blood shed was the sacrificial offering and atonement for

every sin that could ever be committed. Did you hear me?

You must understand that the blood of Jesus is efficacious!

Meaning, that the blood of Jesus is the *remedy* for the

blotting out of sin in the sight of God. Jesus' blood is so

powerful, it heals, saves, delivers, and set the captives free. It

covers all sin, no matter the offence.

Without the shedding of His blood, there is no

remission or removing of our sin according to scripture. We

would remain guilty! The judgement of God would cause us to Perish. Now, this alone should make every person, and especially those who are born again, at minimum, completely thankful. Oh, and let me add that the blood of Jesus is our hiding place from evil and the devil. When you pray, it is quite alright to ask God to cover you and your family under the blood of Jesus!

See, it is only the blood and the word of God that cleanses us from the very stench of sin. In the olden days, the people had to find acceptable animals that could be offered up to God for the forgiveness of sin.

1 John 1:10 says, "if we say we have not sinned, we make Him a liar, and His word is not in us. For all have sinned and fall short of the glory of God." There is nothing that we can do of ourselves to get right with His Majesty. We must

come through the way that was made, and Jesus is the way, the truth, and the life. Can you imagine having to go out and find an unblemished lamb, goat or turtledove, and then pray that the man who is standing as the bridge between you and God himself is sanctified and found worthy before the Almighty God to offer up a sacrifice for the forgiveness of your sins? And at the pace of the growing population that we now live in, in combination with the amount of sin we as people commit all day, every day against God, we would not have enough animals. So, Jesus became that perfect sacrifice for us and did away with all of that for us. What a Mighty God we serve!In depth, the blood of Jesus is a covering, an eternal covenant, a protection, a cleanser, and a purchaser! His blood purchased our salvation. Hallelujah! His blood is alive and active in the believer's life. Scripture references: Matthew 26:26-30; Mark 14:22-25; and Luke 22:14-20.

Daphne Y. Mitchell

In 1 Corinthians 11:23-29; Paul the Apostle writes,

> For I received from the Lord that which I also
> delivered to you; that the Lord Jesus on the same
> night in which He was betrayed took bread; and when
> He had given thanks, He broke it and said, "Take eat;
> this is my body which is broken for you; do this in
> remembrance of me." In the same manner He also
> took the cup after supper, saying, "This cup is the new
> covenant in my blood. This do, as often as you drink
> it, in remembrance of me." For as often as you eat
> this bread and drink this cup, you proclaim the Lord's
> death till He comes. Therefore, whoever eats this
> bread and drinks this cup of the Lord in an unworthy
> manner will be guilty of the body and blood of the
> Lord. But let a man examine himself, and so let him
> eat of the bread and drink of the cup. For he who eats
> and drinks in an unworthy manner eats and drinks
> damnation to himself, not discerning the Lord's body.

When we utterly understand that a death took

place to spare each of us individually, and that we must

accept Him into our hearts by faith, we commune with the

right perspective. We are communing with Jesus in the

communion service because we are partaking of His body

and His blood! For this cause, we will not eat and drink

unworthy because we are careful to please our Lord in our everyday lives by forsaking those things that He hates and names as sin.

Furthermore, you should know that it is written that if we eat and drink the Lord's body unworthily, many now are weak and sick, and fall asleep (1 Corinthians 11:17).

This sleep can be both spiritual and physical. This is a sacred time of worship and should never be tampered with, period. And at the same time, if you do not partake of the Lord's body and His blood, He said, "You will have no life in you" (John 6:53).

I am remembering the mighty words written by Benny Hinn, "When we are washed by His blood and cleansed by the Word, then the Lord puts the seal of the Holy Spirit on us.

Paul writes:

> In Him you also trusted, after you heard the
> word of truth, the gospel of your salvation;
> in whom also, having believed, you were
> sealed with the Holy Spirit of promise, who
> is the guarantee of our inheritance until the
> redemption of the purchased possession, to the
> praise of His glory.

Ephesians 1:13-14

Additionally, Mr. Hinn goes on to say, "I never conduct a service without thanking Him for the blood. And every time I do, the presence of God descends, and miracles take place. In the Old Covenant, God responded with fire when blood was offered on the alter. So, it is today, when the blood of Jesus is honored, when the cross is honored, the Holy Spirit comes and touches people's lives."

We used to sing a song in church and the words are so powerful – "some through the water, some through the flood, but all must go through the blood."

Hell is Greedy For Souls

As this chapter closes, it is my prayer that you have read something that pricked your heart and enlightened your eyes to the anguish, the agony, the bitter sorrow of death that Jesus went through just for you and me. He prayed for this bitter cup to pass but His nevertheless, not my will, but thy will be done in the garden of Gethsemane is why you and I owe Him our lives and without measure. His love is serious for us. Do you understand? While we are looking to the things on the earth like Valentine's Day and the right companion to build our lives with, these are temporal fixes for a void that only God can truly fill. It is a wonderful thing to have a spouse, in fact, God said that it is not good for man to be alone, but these relationships are not eternal, they are temporary. When we die, marriage does not work in Heaven or Hell.

Experience the love of God, bask in the passion of

Christ, and give your life to Him to make and mold. He wants you, that is why He came. There is nothing that you have done that cannot be forgiven, just come on home to the master.

I will lead you: Lord God, thank you for spilling your blood out for me, and Lord, please forgive me of all my sins and trespasses that I have committed against you. Blot out my sins and remember them no more, please have mercy on me. Wash me and make me clean before your sight and help me to live godly unto you in this present world. I choose You, oh God. I believe that you love me and that you died for me, so that I can have a right to the tree of life and be with you for all eternity. I choose You, oh God. Your Word says that if I believe in my heart and confess with my mouth the Lord Jesus, that I would be saved. So, by faith, I believe and confess Jesus Christ as my Savior and now, I am Saved.

Hell is Greedy For Souls

Now, go join a Bible-teaching church and be baptized in the name of Jesus Christ for the remission of your sin and you will receive the gift of the Holy Ghost (Acts 2:38).

Amen! Welcome to the family of God. It will not always be easy, but it will always be worth it!

Daphne Y. Mitchell

SIXTH PART

THE SIN ISSUE!

The Word of God says, "But your iniquities have separated between you and your God, and your sins have hidden His face from you that He will not hear" (Isaiah 59:2).

If the issue of sin in your life has not been forgiven by God, you are in grave danger! Get it? Grave Danger. The scripture above says that God has hid His face from you and that He does not even hear you. In fact, John 9:31 says, "Now we know that God heareth not sinners; but if any man be a worshipper of God, and doeth His will, him he heareth."

When we decide to go against the Word of God, we

hinder ourselves tremendously and frustrate the will and

purposes of God for our lives, success, and even the lives and

success of others. It is at close sight that God, through the

death of the man, Jesus, on the cross, does not wish for us to

perish but obtain everlasting life in Him, but only if you want

Him.

Truth be told, we need a shepherd because we do

not know how to take care of ourselves. We often make the

worst choices and go in ways that are not good. The Bible

says that there is a way that seemeth right but the end of it is

destruction. We must ask God for direction to ensure that the

paths we select are going to be profitable for our well-being

with God and man. The Lord says that if we acknowledge

Him in all our ways that He will direct our path. Don't you

desire this?

Hell is Greedy For Souls

It has been proven many times over that those

who stray away from God often end up in a lot of issues,

confusion, and ultimately, Hell. In Luke chapter 16, there is

a rich man who had everything that made his flesh feel good,

but he was not wise. He chose to walk out without God,

and one day death came for him. The Bible says that after

his death, he lifted his eyes in Hell. The scripture records

that he begged for a messenger to be sent to his brothers that

remained alive on the earth. He wanted this messenger to go

and warn his brothers about Hell so that they would not end

up in Hell with him. My question to you is, "Will doing it

your way be worth it?" Your 'it' can be a man or woman that

wants to sleep with you but refuses to make you honorable by

marrying you, or a job that provides great income to you but

never provides you time to read your Bible and go to church

to learn about God and His instructions for living. Perhaps, your 'it' is the pressure of making sure no one calls you soft

for loving Jesus; you may feel that protecting your status with

people and going with the flow is more important. Or your

'it' could be that you don't believe in this Gospel because

there are so many fake people talking about Jesus that the

proof of God seems to be irrelevant at this point. Whatever

your 'it' is, be very sure that not deciding to search for God

and find Him is yielding you a destination that is not going to

be good at all.

Meanwhile, one of the major roots of sin is

selfishness. Selfish people will continually find themselves

trespassing against the laws of God because selfishness is the

seat of sin! You can say, "Amen," or, "Ouch," right here!

James 1:13-15, God says,

Let no man say when he is tempted, I am
tempted of God: for God cannot be tempted
with evil, neither tempteth he any man. But

every man is tempted, when he is drawn away
of his own lust, and enticed. Then when lust
hath conceived, it bringeth forth sin: and sin,
when it is finished, bringeth forth death.

The problem begins with thinking that sin (having

fun) is much more enjoyable than God. Sin is all about

"self"; I want, I feel, I need – which are all the reasons

that most people continue in sin. No one really wants to

deal with a bunch of rules, the do's and the don'ts of life.

Especially when sin feels so good – it calls me, it tempts me,

and it offers me just what I want –but the danger is that we

never consider the large price tag it carries with God. We

spend our lives in this visible world forgetting about the

cloud of witnesses that are in the invisible world listening

to and watching the unlawful words and deeds committed

by mankind. The sin that continually persists in violating

God's Holy Word and has become a stench in His nostrils.

Often, we are not even thankful for the grace, mercy, and longsuffering of God that keeps us from being destroyed all day long.

The assassinator of our souls, satan, our adversary, has strategically come to us with so many ways for us to choose pleasure over God. That devil uses devices, schemes, temptations, plots, and plans that are set in motion by him to derail, rob, and even kill us. The whole mission of the devil is to kill, steal, and destroy. Friends, the trickery of the enemy is real. He wants to hold us as captives and take us at his will so that our chance for salvation will be ruined. The devil means us no good. It is just like falling in love with a man or a woman who never loved you. They just string you along to deplete your heart and good intentions for their own gain and when they are done with you, they throw you away like a piece of trash and never look back. They do not care that you are discarded, that it hurts, that you love them; they

have moved on to the next person as if you never existed.

Here is the thing though, you gave them your everything,

you withheld nothing from them. You thought that you were

pleasing them and that profiting their love was bank! Do

not be deceived. Accept the love of God today and check it

against all other love definitions to see whether it is love!

Love does not hurt or hinder; it comes to give life and life

more abundantly! Ask God to forgive you for leaving His

presence, His ways, and desperately cry out to Him to save

you from your sins! He is willing and He is able. Hallelujah!

In wrapping up this part, 2 Timothy 3:1-7, God says,

> In the last days, perilous times shall come.
> For men shall become lovers of their
> own selves, covetous, boasters, proud,
> blasphemers, disobedient to parents,
> unthankful and unholy. Without natural
> affection, trucebreakers, false accusers,
> incontinent, fierce, despisers of those that are
> good. Traitors, heady, high-minded, lovers

of pleasures more than lovers of God. Having a form of godliness but denying the power thereof, from such turn away. For of this sort are they which creep into houses and lead captive silly women laden with sins, led away with divers' lust. Ever learning, and never able to come to the knowledge of the truth.

2 Timothy 3:13 says, "but evil men and seducers shall wax worse and worse, deceiving and being deceived."

Listen, we have all fallen short of the glory of God, but it is past time to turn back to God and repent. Be born again, read the best book on the planet and pray that your name will be found in the Lamb's Book of Life! Selah!

SEVENTH PART

WHAT IN HELL DO YOU WANT

Hell is not a popular topic in today's world and

therefore it is not talked about regularly in the church or

even mentioned in some new versions of the Bible. A lot

of preachers choose to gratify the people's ear and give

them words that comfort and tell them how good God is

to them, despite their sin. And there is no way, they will

rattle the cage by preaching the whole gospel of Jesus

Christ because of the potential financial loss and because

membership numbers will fall drastically. It is very similar

to the COVID-19 pandemic, states are opening up places that

hold mass crowds because the world needs to have a healthy economy despite the fact that bodies are still being thrown in the back of U-Haul trucks because mortuaries can no longer take those dead corpse. Forgetting that these corpses all had souls that might now be in the grips of an evil devil's Hell, but hopefully resting in the bosom of Abraham in paradise. We will never truly know!

Hell is not a party station where they are singing, "let it burn, we do not give a heck, let the fire burn." No, they are weeping, screaming, wailing, and gnashing their teeth. Millions of people are begging for a drop of water for their tongue because they are being burned day and night. The tears are pouring out of me right now because of the possibility of my loved one's going to this place, and there will be no hope of them ever getting out of this place. The residents of Hell are wishing that they could have one more chance to repent and turn back to God, but it will not happen.

God said that those who forget Him will be turned into Hell!

Immediately after death comes the judgement. Either the

person that dies has just entered paradise or Hell! What in

Hell do you want from Hell? I'll wait!

A lot of people teach that Hell is not a physical place,

so let me inform you that these are deceivers amongst you.

They are lying, and the truth is not in them. The Bible warns

us that in the heart of this earth, souls are on fire! Psalms

86:13 says, "For great is thy mercy toward me and thou hast

delivered my soul from the lowest hell." This means that

there are levels to Hell and Job 11:8 says, that "Hell is deep."

Psalms 116:3 says, "The sorrows of death compassed me,

and the pains of Hell gat hold upon me, I found trouble and

sorrows."

WHAT DID JESUS SAY ABOUT HELL?

He said, it is better for some part of your body

to perish than for your whole body to be cast into Hell.

Therefore, Jesus was not talking about the grave. He

is talking about an eternal place full of the wrath and

indignation of God because of sin. There is no hope outside

of Christ, please get worried so that you can get delivered.

Do not walk away from this book thinking that you have

time. You may not, you could be suddenly called out of this

life and all that you have done will not matter. There is a

reward that has our names on it! A reward with full payment

for the good and evil deeds committed by us.

Before the Lord returns to rapture His bride (the

church), there are going to be many sorrows in this land.

He says in Matthew chapter 24, that there will be wars and

rumors of wars, earthquakes in many places, betrayals of

family members, many false prophets rising up, a lot of

hatred, persecution of believers in Christ will be afflicted and

killed for His names sake. The love of many will wax cold!

Famines and pestilences will take hold of the land, which is

either here or coming, what will you do? The scripture is

fulfilling and many of you are still not saved. Saved from

what? Saved from Hell and destruction. The only way to be

saved is that there must be a Savior, and the only Savior is

Jesus Christ.

See, there is a way which seemeth right to a man, but

the end thereof are the ways of death (Proverbs 14:12).

With so many choices and the power of free will, a

person can choose to go any path they want to. For example,

a person can choose to live free in the earth or they can

choose to be bound. A choice can be made to have one wife

or many wives, one husband or many husbands, you can

be rich or poor, fat or skinny. Notice, the operative word is

"choice."

Now, even though God has given us the power to

choose, if our choices do not line up with the Word of God,

then we are definitely not in the will of God, because God's

Word is God's will.

With today's technology and knowledge, coupled

with the lust of the eyes, the lust of the flesh, and the pride of

life, our choices are endless, it would seem. Really, there is a

lot one person could get into if left to his or her imagination.

Having twenty-four hours a day to drink alcohol, do drugs,

have unrestrained sex with as many humans that are willing,

eat foods flown in from around the world if you can afford

it, shop for the latest and greatest styles, travel from city to

country and all at the moment of a decision. We can use our

fingertips to type our thoughts into our computers and make

things happen, right in the comfort of our living rooms.

And even if a person cannot live a lavish life, the choice to

fall somewhere in the middle and enjoy some of the things

mentioned above are possible. In fact, all the way down

to the poorest person, choices are being made. Choices to

become a serial rapist, a serial killer, a professional robber, or

perhaps a vagabond and just wander and beg. is all a choice.

It is only through the providence of God that we have

hopefully been predestined to return to Him. The Bible

speaks of only two paths. The path of righteousness, which

is defined as narrow and only a few find this path, and then

there is the wide path, this is the path of wickedness and

there be many that walk therein. The wide path leads to

destruction of one's self! And a bigger problem is that the journey is not always obvious, so it is only at death when that person lifts their eyes in Hell that they discover their damnation. It is not only full of the torments of Hell, but it is the forever state of that soul because repentance does not work after death. The reward of your path is sealed!

Right now, you can repent for all your sins and ask God to forgive you and come in your life and rule; He will have mercy on you if you mean it.

Now, let us talk about what is the will or way of God so that there will not be any confusion.

First, you must believe that God is God and that He is a rewarder to those who diligently seek after Him. Now, repent for your sins and ask for forgiveness, then confess with your mouth that Jesus Christ is Lord and you will be saved. Now, ask God to fill you with His Holy Spirit.

As you read earlier in the beginning of this short book, that God gave ten commandments which are really summed up in these two: (1) love the Lord God with all your mind, soul, and body, and have no other gods before Him, and (2) love your neighbor as yourself. See, if you love God the way He tells us to love Him, you will cherish your relationship with Him and will not be willing to forsake His path for your life. Also, if we love our neighbor as we love ourselves, we will not do anyone any form of hurt; would not this world be a peaceful and bountiful place to live?

Galatians chapter 5 speaks to us about the two paths clearly as well. Let's look at the behaviors and deeds of a person on the narrow path first and then let's examine the behaviors and deeds of the person on the wide path which is completely out of the will and way of God.

NARROW PATH: Galatians 5:14 – Love your neighbor as

yourself.

WIDE PATH: Galatians 5:19–21 says,

> Now the works of the flesh are manifest,
> which are these, adultery, fornication,
> uncleanness, lasciviousness. Idolatry,
> witchcraft, hatred, variance, emulations,
> wrath, strife, seditions, heresies, envying's,
> murders, drunkenness, revellings, and such
> like; of which I told you in time past, that
> they which do such things shall not inherit the
> kingdom of God.

By our living, the scriptures expose what manner of person

we are through our thoughts, deeds, and actions. Selah!

EIGHTH PART

THE FAITH WALK

Hebrews 11:1, "Now Faith is the substance of things hoped for, the evidence of things not seen."

That means if you can see what you hope for, why are you hoping, just go ahead and get it. Faith is hoping for what you cannot see! It is believing that what I hope for, I, by faith in God, will receive it! Our faith in God must be so ferocious that nothing can penetrate it! You and I must believe in God so much that it amazes God Himself! This faith *does* exist, for we see it in the life of others as told in the Bible, and we can see it amongst some of the brethren in this present world.

But guess what, we can also see it in our lives if we believe.

Hallelujah!

Abraham, the man of faith, believed God until God called him His friend! Did you hear me? God called Abraham, His friend. This amazes me because God is the God of the universe, and He looked at His relationship with Abraham in such an affectionate way by *claiming* him as a friend of His! Powerful!

Meanwhile over 4,350 years ago, Noah, by faith, believed God and built an Ark during a time on the earth where it had never rained from the sky, but God would water the earth from below the earth. So when Noah began to build the Ark, I can imagine that the people of his day must have mocked him terribly. They probably thought to themselves, *This man has gone wild in his mind. He and his family have checked out*. They were probably laughing at him and calling him all types of names, but Noah did not waiver from his faith. Noah was obedient to the instructions of God despite the mocking and despite the laughing. The Bible tells us that God gave Noah specific instructions and measurements on how to build the Ark, and those instructions included a timeline for him to move with haste, which means to hurry up and get it done! This massive ship was 510 feet long, 85 feet wide, and 51 feet high and housed Noah and his family, plus two of every kind of beast that was on the face of the earth. God saved those that believed in Him and enough animals of every kind to replenish the earth once the Ark landed! It is astonishing to know that the Ark was built to save the people that heeded to the warnings of Noah's voice, but because they would not, animals took their place. Everyone but Noah and his family died in a watery grave. The book of Genesis, chapters 6 and 7, are where you can read the entire truth of God's Word concerning Noah and the Lord's Ark of Safety.

Let us be clear: without faith, it is impossible to please God. The scripture says in Hebrews 11:6 that if a person would come to God, he must first believe that God is God and that God is a rewarder of those who diligently seek Him. God must be believed at all cost, and that is the bottom line! God is not a liar, but the devil is! God says what He means, and He means what He says. Period!

Now that you have seen some examples of faith in action, you may be wondering on how you can get this type of faith, or how you might increase your faith. I am happy to show you the way. God says, "Faith cometh by hearing, and hearing by the word of God" (Romans 10:17).

So, in other words, you and I cannot obtain faith unless

we hear God's Word, and trust it against every other thought, imagination, and fact known under the sun. God's Word is God! And God is immutable and can never be changed!

When we hear God's Word and believe it by applying it to our everyday lives, God's Word will begin to transform our lives from our own ways to the ways of God. See, the only way to know that you are really hearing God's Word is by how it takes root in you. If it is rooted in you, it will transform you and you will be shaped into His living epistle! The Bible is the living epistle, and your life will be a constant reflection of it. Because the words in the Bible are alive and active, when we read or hear them, faith is activated! In the natural, anything that you do all the time, or whatever you practice, you become. For example, a man or woman that exercises all the time, begins to transform into a more muscular and fit person, right? Likewise, a person that runs all the time will transform into a person that has a lot of stamina and endurance. While

a person that eats a lot of junk food becomes heavier in their

weight and often-times develops laziness and sicknesses, like

diabetes and high blood pressure. What we practice is what we

become. So, become alive in your faith and fight for it!

When it comes to faith, I will not deceive you, once

you make your mind up that you are going to truly give your

life to God and live in Him, there will be many people who

will come up against your faith. There will be satan the old

serpent there to tempt your faith, there will be your own flesh

there to test your faith, and oh yes, there will be God Himself,

there to prove your faith. It will seem impossible to overcome

sometimes, but I am a witness that you can! God's Word is

given to us to study, we should fall in love with the scroll, so

that when trials and testing of life come up, we will be armed

with the Word of God. And our faith will become the shield

that quenches every fiery dart of the enemy and the enemies

of Christ.

Our faith acts just like a key, and in fact, our faith is

key! For example, you can have a car, but it cannot be entered

without the key, the key gives legal access to the car. Our faith

gives us legal access to God, and God rewards those who have

faith in Him.

Making up our minds to do things the way God says

always brings about immediate opposition and spiritual

attacks. There is an evil force that fights against the godly

who are in the way! Paul, our beloved brother in the gospel of

Jesus Christ said,

> I find then a law, that, when I would do good,
> evil is present with me. For I delight in the law
> of God after the inward man, but I see another
> law in my members, warring against the law of
> my mind, and bringing me into captivity to the
> law of sin which is in my members. O wretched
> man that I am! Who shall deliver me from the
> body of this death? I thank God through Jesus

Christ our Lord. So then with the mind I myself serve the law of God, but with the flesh the law of sin.

Romans 7:21-25

This scripture is a testimony that if we do not keep the law of God in our minds, our flesh will win every time! The mind vs. the flesh, day after day after day! Our thought pattern is critical in illuminating our master. Selah!

God said, "No one can serve two masters, for either he will hate the one, and love the other; or else he will hold to the one and despise the other. Ye cannot serve God and mammon" (Matthew 6:24). (Mammon represents flesh.)The reason for sharing all the above is that it is a testament to how our faith will be tried and why it is tried. It is always the assassinators job to discredit God, and how can he do that? The devil comes up against our knowledge of God and repeatedly attempts to decrease our faith in God. He thinks that by sending the weapons of Hell against us, that we will give up on God, that we will shut up and give up! But we who believe will never leave God or God's way!

Personally, my faith has been put on trial more times then I care to remember, but through it all, I have found grace with God to overcome. I remember when my son's dad and I were trying to purchase our first home, the mortgage company rejected our loan application. I refused to believe that God, my heavenly father, owns the world and that we could not have a small lot. I refused to have that mortgage company make me believe their words over God's Word. We were tithers and faithful to God. I said to myself, *Go back to God in prayer, rehearse what He says to us in the area of faith, get the yellow pages and contact every mortgage company in the book, and apply for a loan.* Finally, one day, we got a letter from a different mortgage company stating that they could approve the loan, and ironically, the original mortgage company who

told us, "No," called to say, "Yes!" We watched our first home

be built from the ground up and moved into a beautiful home

in Lithonia, Georgia. Serving God in spirit and truth and

believing Him does pay off! But faith without works is dead!

However, if we combine the Word of God with our faith and

our actions, the results will always be victorious!

ARMOUR UP SOLDIER!

Ephesians 6:10-18 says,

> Finally my brethren, be strong in the Lord, and in the power of His might. Put on the whole armour of God, that ye may be able to stand against the wiles of the devil. For we wrestle not against flesh and blood, but against principalities, against powers, against the rulers of the darkness of this world, against spiritual wickedness in high places. Wherefore take unto you the whole armour of God, that ye may be able to withstand in the evil day, and having done all, to stand. Stand therefore, having your loins girt about with truth, and having on the breastplate of righteousness; And your feet shod with the preparation of the gospel of peace; Above all, taking the shield of faith, wherewith ye shall be able to quench all the fiery darts of the wicked. And take the helmet of salvation and the word of God, praying always with all prayer and supplication in the Spirit, and watching thereunto with all perseverance and supplication for all saints.

You must get dressed and stay dressed. The writer starts by saying, "put on," that is an actionable command that each of us must do for our own selves! If you will read and study the Word of God, go to church, and get involved with the things of

God up under a God fearing pastor, pray to God daily, meditate

on His Word, you will have good success, and your faith will

increase more and more. Stay away from things and people

that oppose your faith, lest you become entangled again and a

yoke of bondage grab you by the neck to hold you down from

being set free in Christ Jesus.

NINTH PART

THE RAPTURE!

What is the Rapture? The Holy Bible declares to us

that God will rapture His bride. Let us talk about it in depth.

May the Lord open your eyes and understanding now, for you

do not want to miss this and be left behind.

The rapture is explained in 1 Thessalonians 4:13-17,

and it says,

> But I would not have you to be ignorant,
> brethren, concerning them which are asleep,
> that ye sorrow not, even as others which have
> not hope. For if we believe that Jesus died
> and rose again, even so them also which sleep
> in Jesus will God bring with him. For this we
> say unto you by the word of the Lord, that we
> which are alive and remain unto the coming
> of the Lord shall not prevent them which are

asleep. For the Lord himself shall descend from heaven with a shout, with the voice of the archangel, and with the trump of God: and the dead in Christ shall rise first: Then we which are alive and remain shall be caught up together   with them in the clouds, to meet the Lord in the air: and so shall we ever be with the Lord.

Now in unpacking this scripture, let me set things in order for the time and season that we are currently living in. Jesus told us to take heed that no man deceives us! That in the last days, perilous times would come! And dear reader, perilous times are here! Because Jesus loves us with an amazing and faithful love, He takes the time to include in the scriptures the gift of forewarning, letting us know what things will start to happen as His next appearance gets closer; that appearing is known as "The Rapture" or "First Resurrection."He tells His servants to share with us these signs and the signs are evident all around us that the coming of Jesus is extremely near.

Hell is Greedy For Souls

Listen to this, 2 Peter 3:9-11 says,

> The Lord is not slack concerning HIS
> promise, as some men count slackness; but
> is longsuffering to us-ward, not willing that
> any should perish, but that all should come
> to repentance. But the day of the Lord will
> come as a thief in the night; in the which the
> heavens shall pass away with a great noise,
> and the elements shall melt with fervent
> heat, the earth also and the works that are
> therein shall be burned up. Seeing then
> that all these things shall be dissolved, what
> manner of persons ought ye to be in all holy
> conversations and godliness.

Looking for and hasting unto the coming of the day of God,

wherein the Heavens being on fire shall be dissolved, and the

elements shall melt with fervent heat?

In making this concrete,

2 Timothy 3:1-5 says,

> This know also, that in the last days perilous
> times shall come. For men shall be lovers
> of their own selves, covetous, boasters,
> proud, blasphemers, disobedient to parents,
> unthankful, unholy. Without natural affection,
> trucebreakers, false accusers, incontinent,
> fierce, despisers of those that are good.
> Traitors, heady, high-minded, lovers of

pleasures more than lovers of God; Having
a form of godliness but denying the power
thereof; from such turn away.

Now unless you are in a coma, surely you can agree with

the Bible right here. People are fulfilling the scriptures

right before our very eyes. We see the fierceness of people

every day increasing so that it is not safe to leave any door

unlocked. It's not wise to be unaware of your surroundings;

we must pay to alarm our homes, put cameras everywhere,

and even in the congregation of church goers, people are now

entering with guns to shoot and kill innocent people right in

the church house. The fierceness of unholy and unthankful

people is so bad that even some who wear the cloth in the

pulpit are stealing money, having sex with the church goers,

teaching that it is okay to create another doctrine apart from

God's statutes, judgements, and ordinances. Telling people

that it is okay to be gay, it is okay to shack up and fornicate,

Hell is Greedy For Souls

it is okay to sin and just ask for forgiveness later. The times

are so bad that people are killing members of their own

families and burying them in the backyard or stuffing them

into refrigerators; some will even go as far as to eat the

deceased body. Children do not listen to their parents and

will even fight them. Policemen who are being paid to serve

and protect are being arrested for brutality and murder of

the citizens they are sworn to protect, and in a lot of cases,

some of these people are dying because of the hatred that

lies within the heart of a badged racist. Demons are on an

all-out rampage! Meanwhile, the elements around us are

also speaking! We are having earthquakes in diverse areas,

twirling winds of tornadic descent popping up more than

ever, whirlwinds of horrific magnitude in hurricanes like

never before, forest fires give us a good glimpse of what

Hell-fire resembles, sink holes are swallowing houses with

people in them, wild animals are coming out to homes with aggression to devour people even though we should have dominion over them. We are living in a time that people who are supposed to make righteous calls are calling evil 'good' and good 'evil.' The judgement of mankind is off the Richter scale. People are losing hope, jobs, spouses, children, friendships, health battles, houses, and their minds, and the church who has the remedy is sitting at home minding their very own business. Some are not one bit concerned about the needs of the people, and because of this, we can see the reason why a great falling away from the church is happening. Self-perseverance is not what the Gospel of Jesus Christ is about, in fact, Jesus says that if you will save your life, you will lose it, but if you will lose your life for His sake and the sake of the Gospel, you will find your life and live.

Bear with me while I tie this together now!

C

Hell is Greedy For Souls

Summary of events: Jesus is going to come and take away the faith believing church which is known as His bride. He will do this in a moment that is unannounced like a thief in the night. This is called the rapture or First Resurrection, blessed are those who are caught up in the First Resurrection (Revelation 20:6).

Now while we who are caught up are at the Marriage Supper in Heaven with Christ, this will be taking place on earth: Pay Attention!

In Matthew chapter 24, Jesus warns that many false people will begin to come claiming that they are Him, that they are Christ. He says, "Do not be deceived." He warns that there will be wars and rumor of wars, that nation will rise up against nation and kingdom against kingdom, that there will be famines, pestilences, earthquakes in diverse places and that all of this is the beginning of sorrows. He says that many new believers during this time will be delivered up to be afflicted and killed, and that those believers will be hated by all nations because of Him. Because of the stress of the time in the land, people will begin to hate one another and betray and offend one another. While at the same time, false prophets are going to rise and begin to deceive many. Because wickedness is going to be so great, the love of many people will grow cold, and even though the gospel will continue to be preached, many will fall away from the faith and choose to forsake God's truths.

If you are left behind, you can still make it in, but you will go through seven years of tribulation where you will have to endure great persecutions to be saved.

Reader, the Beginning of Sorrows is the prelude to the *Great*

Hell is Greedy For Souls

Tribulation!

This, is why your faith walk is so important now! Therefore,

the book of 1 Peter 1:7-9, says,

> That the trial of your faith, being much more
> precious than of gold that perisheth, though
> it be tried with fire, might be found unto
> praise and honour and glory at the appearing
> of Jesus Christ. Whom having not seen, ye
> love; in whom though now ye see him not, yet
> believing, ye rejoice with joy unspeakable and
> full of glory. Receiving the end of your faith,
> even the salvation of your souls.

And why our brother Paul the Apostle wrote to Titus this:

Titus 2:11-13 says,For the grace of God that bringeth

salvation hath appeared unto all men. Teaching us that

denying ungodliness and worldly lusts, we should live

soberly, righteously, and godly, in this present world;

Looking for that blessed hope and the glorious appearing of

the great God and our Savior Jesus Christ.

Can you now see why the enemy wants to destroy your faith?

If he can steal your faith, he will steal your seat in Heaven.

Remember, he got kicked out and does not want you to have

Heaven with God, but instead Hell and Hell-fire with him

in torments. Again, I ask you what in the Hell do want from

Hell? Do not make that choice and do not keep quiet about

this Gospel of Jesus Christ. It has the power of God to save

all them that believe.

Meanwhile, why is Jesus taking His bride away

for seven (7) years? What will we be doing while the great

tribulation is happening on earth?

I am glad you asked. The Rapture is not for show;

it is the honeymoon for the believers. We are going back to

what is known as the "Marriage Supper of the Lamb." Hear

the word of the Lord:

> And I heard as it were the voice of a great
> multitude, and as the voice of many waters,
> and as the voice of mighty thunderings,

saying, "Alleluia: for the Lord God omnipotent reigneth. Let us be glad and rejoice and give honour to Him: for the marriage of the Lamb is come, and His wife hath made herself ready. And to her was granted that she should be arrayed in fine linen, clean and white; for the fine linen is the righteousness of saints." And He saith unto me, "Write Blessed are they which are called unto the marriage supper of the Lamb." And He saith unto me, "These are the true sayings of God."

Revelation 19:6-9

This is the Glorious celebration we must look forward to, so while we are suffering here as believers because it seems like we are faithful but forsaken, know that there is a day coming where the redeemed of the Lord will celebrate!

Do not miss out on this celebration trying to keep up with this worldly mindset of gaining money and fame; it is all about to be burned. If friends, spouses, family members, church members, and so on forsake you, let them go! Thank you, Bishop T.D. Jakes, for setting the tone in a message that you preached on just how to let them go! Ask for the gift

of 'Good-Bye!' If your mother, father, sister, brother, bestie,

spouse, children, and what- or whoever leaves or is lost, just

count it as dung for the excellency of Him that is coming.

We cannot force people to see what we see. What we can do,

is fast and pray that their eyes be opened along with their

understanding, and that either way, we will not give up our

celebration invite, which is the redemption of our souls and

an eternal stay with our God! Hallelujah and Amen!

LAST PART

THE GREAT TRIBULATION!

Blessed be the rock of my salvation! Hosanna

blessed be the rock of my salvation! I praise God that I will

not be here to go through this! This is that scary! The scary

that John on the Isle of Patmos fell on his face as a dead man

saw when God began to show him what would happen!

If you are not already dead or caught up in the

Rapture or the First Resurrection, and you go through this

great tribulation, here is what your will suffer.

The seals, the trumpets, the books, the beast, the two

witnesses, the vials, and the judgement. He that hath an ear let him hear what the spirit saith unto the church!

HISTORY: John was exiled on an ancient version of Alcatraz, but God was with him and began to give him visions of the future. On this small island of Patmos, John was worshipping when he hears the voice of God and as he turns to the voice, he records that he sees Jesus. Let me peel it back for you. Be mindful to listen to what you are reading and try to imagine this in your mind. Take it seriously, as it is the written Word of God and it will happen. God says, "Blessed are those who keepeth the sayings of the prophecy of this book" (Revelation 22:7).

Beginning in the book of Revelation, the first chapter, God is still talking with the bride before He shows up to her. God says, "judgement will begin at the house of God" (1 Peter 4:17).

Hell is Greedy For Souls

In Revelation chapters 1-4, He is showing us what He

is for and what He is against as it relates to the church, and

He affords us the opportunity to clean up our acts and repent!

He is warning us through different examples of what His

view from Heaven looks like when He looks at the church.

The Lord says to John:

I am Alpha and Omega, the first and the last:
and, What thou seest, write in a book, and
send it unto the seven churches which are
in Asia; unto Ephesus, and unto Smyrna,
and unto Pergamos, and unto Thyatira, and
unto Sardis, and unto Philadelphia, and unto
Laodicea.

Revelation 1:11

Because God knows our works, He begins to expose

us on a deeper level and let us in on us! He begins to tell us

the things that He has against us and enlightens us on the fate

of all who will not repent and re-do their first works over.

He also shows us the fate of the devil. God admonishes us

who have an ear to hear, to hear what the Spirit saith unto the churches.

But as we move into the fifth and remaining chapters, the word of God begins to reveal these moments in time where things that have never been seen begin to happen. In the sixth chapter, the first seal was opened, and John heard a loud noise of thunder, and one of the beasts saying, "Come and see." And John saw a white horse and he that sat on him had a bow; and a crown was given unto him and he went forth conquering, and to conquer.

The second seal was then opened and there went out a red horse whose rider was given the power to take away peace from the earth, and cause the people of the earth to kill one another, and the rider carried a great sword. The third seal was opened, and a black horse was shown, and its rider had a pair of balances in his hand, while the fourth seal was

being opened and a pale horse was seen and its rider whose

name is Death, and Hell followed with him. And power

was given unto them over the fourth part of the earth, to kill

with the sword, and with hunger, and with death, and with

the beasts of the earth. And when the fifth seal was opened,

John saw under the altar the souls of them that were slain

for the Word of God, and for the testimony which they held.

And they were crying out with a loud voice, saying, "How

long, O Lord, holy and true, dost thou not judge and avenge

our blood on them that dwell on the earth?" When the sixth

seal was opened, there was a great earthquake, and the sun

became black as sackcloth of hair, and the moon became as

blood. And the stars of Heaven fell unto the earth, and the

Heaven departed as a scroll when it is rolled together; and

every mountain and island were moved out of their places.

This is the great day of Hid wrath and who shall be able to stand? Now, as you can see things are not going to go well from here. The Jews who did not accept Jesus as the Messiah are here, un-repented souls are here, and the lost and damned souls are here on the earth and this is the portion of servings. However, in the seventh chapter, the angel of the Lord says before anything else happens to first go and seal the servants of God in their foreheads. There were sealed a hundred and forty and four thousand of all the tribes of the children of Israel.

There is yet one more seal to be opened, the seventh seal! When it is opened, there will be silence in Heaven about the space of half an hour and then the sounding of the Seven Trumpets will begin. Please take the time to read and be aware of all that will happen here and knowing that these things will take place in the earth. How we must make it our own business not to be left behind. It will not be good here

in the earth during these years but there is yet hope. I will

transition your thoughts now to the hope of God's salvation.

God allowed John in Revelation chapter 21, to see a new

Heaven and a new earth because the Heavens and earth of

today will have already passed away. John says he saw a

holy city, a new Jerusalem, coming down from God out of

Heaven, prepared as a bride adorned for her husband.

In the new Jerusalem, God will dwell with us, there will be

no tears there. No more death, neither sorrow, no more pain,

and everything that we know now, will not be remembered.

God has prepared this for those who love Him. A prepared

city whose gates are of pearl, walls of jasper, pure gold as

crystal clear like unto glass, with foundations of precious

stones. Where there is no need for the sun or the moon

because God Himself will be the light and there is no night

there. There will be kings of this earth, pure rivers of water of life and proceeds from the throne of God. Can you imagine this? The tree of life will be here! Wow!

There will be no need for the police because no murderers, rapists, or evil work will be here. It is Heaven as God intended for His people from the beginning of time. It is a people that chose to die to self and live to God and where we will forever be with Him who loves us. There is no marriage here, none of those fairy tales that we have heard throughout our lives. We will not know our family members like we do today because if we have that mindset, we will cry. We would know that they perished and cry and be sad, but God said there will be no tears here, the former things are all passed away, so He changes us! My God, we shall wear a crown! To enter this city, you are counted as blessed.

Hell is Greedy For Souls

Here is why we must grab a hold of ourselves and repent, do not worry about the wrong that people do to you here. I know it hurts, I know it disappoints, I know it feels unjust, but forgive them, forgive yourself, and move forward. God is a just God and He is the Great Surveillance of the earth; no one will escape from their deeds, no one. So, I would like to take the rest of this time to plea with you and remind myself to submit our ways to God. To really hate sin and the cause and effects of sin! To see the importance of learning about God from the Bible and be quick to be quiet instead of reacting to the things that come along to provoke us unto wrath. We have all sinned and fallen short of the glory of God, but while there is time, we can turn from wickedness and seek the face of God. Be desperate for Him! Ask Him to save your children, your spouses, your siblings, and even your enemies.

Flee youthful lusts of fornication. That means to run from anyone who is tempting you to sin against your body and God. Watch out for the traps that are set to derail you from completing God's assigned task(s) for you, watch out for people who try to attach themselves to you for the purpose of dragging you to Hell with them. These are people who lead or assist you in lying, doing drugs, stealing, committing adultery, for example.

Women, if he has a wife, do not be a partaker with him in sinning against his vows to that woman and God. Men, do not be a partaker of that woman who is opening her gates (her legs) to invite you into the depths of Hell where all her visitors are dead. If you know that the people you hang with are gossipers, do not continue in sin but forsake it! Gossip is a terrible sin and should not be amongst believers.

Know the fruit of a tree! It will be better to be lonely on

this side now than to hang with a bunch of people who are

assigned by the devil to keep you in darkness.

If you have a family, love them and pray for them!

Watch out for their souls with fasting and prayer. We have

to do more to see different results, we do not experience all

that God has for us because we do not put the time in to the

ways of God to get the results that we so desperately need.

Really, we would be mourning more if we utterly understood

that the Bible is the truth and this world is a big lie, with all

its illusions of fame and prosperity. What profit is it to gain

power and prestige just to have a mosquito come and bite

you, poison you, and watch you die. It is that simple, a tiny

mosquito could have an assignment to take us out of here

suddenly. We must prioritize the seconds of our minutes in

this earth. It is so serious, and we must wonder why God

allowed COVID-19 to happen? COVID-19 for me was one

of the realest times of my life as it relates to enlightening.

The mandate to shelter in place, cover up your mouth and your nose, and wash your hands! When I thought about covering up my mouth and my nose, all that remained out were my eyes and my ears for the top portion of my body! Come on with me, my eyes allow me to see and my ears allow me to hear, but the mask was placed over my nose and my mouth! Symbolically, I see that as a message to be quiet and watch! Be quiet and listen! All while keeping your hands clean! I think that God uses situations for us to learn from, and when we miss valuable lessons, we are at high risk to perish. Shelter in place with your family—I believe that God has given us an opportunity to really spend more time with one another and appreciate each other. He afforded us an opportunity to save money, save time, get some rest, all while shifting is taking place. People, jobs, establishments are all wondering what their fate will be. God help us.

This foreshadow of things to come is an awakening for a lot of people and yet there are those whose eyes remain glued shut while appearing open. Here is where we can all begin to intercede. Let us build an altar to God as families and seek Him while it is day, for the night is coming where no man can work. Every day, we can go to God without hindrance, we can go to Him in sincere prayer and with a joyful heart knowing that He died for us because He loves us and loves it when we rely on Him as our salvation. The Lord is our salvation, He saves our souls, our lives, our minds, our health, our everything. He makes a point about churches during this pandemic too. He affords us to see just how lazy people are concerning the things of God. Many people went to their jobs that the world called essential, including myself because I work in healthcare, but the most essential place on earth should be the presence of God in the House of God. If we can put on a mask and go to the grocery store, gas station, work, then why couldn't the doors of the church be opened? We saw some pastors open the parking lots for people to come out and worship in their cars, and we thank God for their faithfulness. But I am reminded that throughout the history of the church, we saw the saints be nailed to a post and set on fire to give light for the romans. Remember, under the rule of the Emperor Nero, who even had his own power hungered mother killed, he ruled for less than two decades, having Christians fed to lions and burning their bodies in the garden of his courts while he had parties – all because of their faith. Christians even under that great pressure continued steadfast with God and we could not even put on a face mask and go to the house of God? Yes, look at what is going on around us, look at what is going on in us. Let a man examine his own self and see what you can do to assist God

in pointing others to Christ Jesus before it is too late.

How can the world make a distinction between

the church and them if we do what they do and talk their

language? Bitter and sweet water cannot come out of the

same fountain. Let us continue to learn about God and stay

sweet in the Lord until He raptures us out of here.

One last thing: Whatever you do, do not take the mark of the

beast!

Revelation 13:16-18

"The beast required everyone – small and great,

rich and poor, free and slave – to be given a mark on the

right hand or on the forehead. And no one could buy or sell

anything without that mark."

Okay, this will happen during the great tribulation

days, and as you can see, the devil is not an original, but a

falsehood! He is so lost and ruined but puts forth his best

to try and mimic God's plan. Word to the wise: watch those

who mimic you! You will know the tree by the fruit it bears.

And be sure that no man deceives you, the Bible clearly

states where the mark of the beast will be placed, and that it

will be the number 666.

"Here is wisdom. Let him that hath understanding count the

number of a man; and his number is Six hundred threescore

and six." It is obvious that if you take the mark of the beast

that you do not belong to God. And yet, if you are left behind

during this time, you will not be able to buy or sale anything

and that hunger and death will be eminent, but if you endure,

you will overcome.

The angel of the Lord in Revelation 14:9-11 says,

> And the third angel followed them, saying
> with a loud voice, if any man worship the
> beast and his image, and receive his mark in
> his forehead or his hand. The same shall drink
> of the wine of the wrath of God, which is
> poured out without mixture into the cup of his
> indignation; and he shall be tormented with
> fire and brimstone in the presence of the holy
> angels, and in the presence of the Lamb. And
> the smoke of their torment ascendeth up for
> ever and ever; and they have no rest day nor
> night, who worship the beast and his image,
> and whosoever receiveth the mark of his
> name.

INVITATION TO SALVATION

WILL YOU GIVE YOUR LIFE TO GOD? IF YOUR ANSWER IS YES,

SAY THIS ALOUD:

Lord God, I have been selfish and unthankful. But now that I know more about you and about your love for me, I repent of my sins, please forgive me, I need you. Thank you for spilling your blood out for me and, Lord, please forgive me of all my sins and trespasses that I have committed against you. Please blot out my sins and remember them no more, have mercy on me. Wash me and make me clean before your sight and help me to live godly unto you in this present world. I choose You, oh God. I believe that you love me and that you died for me, so that I can have a right to the tree of life and be with you for all eternity. I choose You, oh God. Your Word says that if I believe in my heart and confess with my mouth the Lord Jesus, that I would be saved. So, by faith, I believe and confess Jesus Christ as my Savior and now, I am Saved. Rejoice!

Now, go join a Bible-teaching church and be baptized in the name of Jesus Christ for the remission of your sin, and you will receive the gift of the Holy Ghost (Acts 2:38). Amen!

Welcome to the family of God. It will not always be easy, but it will always be worth it!

Daphne Y. Mitchell

AFTERWORD

Lord, I thank you for allowing me to minister to your

people through this book. I ask that you watch over your

sheep and continue to order our steps daily. May those who

gave their lives to you today be surrounded by your angels

like the mountains surround Jerusalem. And thank you for

letting us know that we can never be plucked out of your

hands! In Jesus' mighty name I pray and believe you for the

end time harvest!AMEN!

Daphne Y. Mitchell

ABOUT THE AUTHOR

Daphne has witnessed of and served the Lord Jesus

Christ since 1989 when the Lord called her from a world of

sin and awful shame. Delivering me from a life of drugs

and wretched wickedness, with love and tender mercies, He

drew me into a life of wholeness, holiness, and now presents

me with a cleaner heart and cleaner hands back to Himself.

CXXIX

Now understanding my primary reason for being in the earth, which is to magnify God and His truths; to live a life that is pleasing and that can only be meaningful when basking in His presence and doing what He said to do, "Occupy until I come." I not only seek blessings for myself, but I lay prostrate before God with many tears calling on Him to be merciful to a lost and dying generation. One of my greatest desire is that you not only read this book but share it and that you will repent, get to know about God's love and live for Him. Point others to Him before that great and awful day, the day of the Lord's retribution. Remembering that He has created the wicked for the day of evil (Proverbs 16:4). Amen!

APPENDIX

Romans 5:12

Jeremiah 23:24

Second Part

The Ten Commandments

Deuteronomy 6:4

Exodus 20:5

Third Part

The Report of the Lord

Isaiah 53:1

2 Timothy 3:16-17

Psalms 34:8

John 3:1-7

Acts 2:38

Psalms 9:17

Romans 6:23

Revelation 21:8

Luke 16:22-23

Proverbs 16:4Revelations 4:8

Fourth Part

God's Passionate Love

John 1:1-5

John 1:14

John 3:13-16

Romans 5:8-11

Fifth Part

Power of God's Blood

1 John 1:10

Matthew 26:26-30

Mark 14:22-25

Luke 22:14-20

1 Corinthians 11:23-29

1 Corinthians 11:17

John 6:53

Ephesians 1:13-14

Acts 2:38

Sixth Part

The Sin Issue

Isaiah 59:2

John 9:31

James 1:13-15

2 Timothy 3:1-7

2 Timothy 3:13

Seventh Part

What in HELL do you want?

Psalms 86:13

Job 11:8

Psalms 116:3

Proverbs 14:12

Galatians 5:14

Galatians 5:19-21

Eighth Part

Faith Walk

Hebrews 11:1

Hebrews 11:6

Romans 10:17

Romans 7:21-25

Matthew 6:24

Ephesians 6:10-18

Ninth Part

The Rapture

1 Thessalonians 4:13-17

2 Peter 3:9-11

2 Timothy 3:1-5

Revelation 20:6

Matthew 24

1 Peter 1:7-9

Titus 2:11-13

Revelation 19:6-9

Last Part

Great Tribulation

Revelation 22:7

1 Peter 4:17

Revelation 1-4

Revelation 1:11

Revelation 21

Revelation 13:16-18

Revelation 14:9-11

Acts 2:38

Proverbs 16:4

Daphne Y. Mitchell

Bibliography

Benny Hinn, *The Blood, It's Power from Genesis to Jesus to You* (Orlando, Fla,: Creation House, 1993), p. 154.

Holman Bible Publishers, <u>The Holy Bible in the King James Version</u>, Nashville Tennessee, 1998.

Daphne Y. Mitchell

CPSIA information can be obtained
at www.ICGtesting.com
Printed in the USA
LVHW010436220221
679515LV00004B/609